DH Lawrence, The Poetry

Poetry is a fascinating use of language. With almost a million words at its command it is not surprising that these Isles have produced some of the most beautiful, moving and descriptive verse through the centuries. In this series we look at individual poets who have shaped and influenced their craft and cement their place in our heritage.

For many of us DH Lawrence was a schoolboy hero. Who can forget sniggering in class at the mention of Women In Love or Lady Chatterley's Lover? Lawrence was a talented if nomadic writer whose novels were passionately received, suppressed at times and generally at odds with Establishment values. This of course did not deter him. At his death in 1930 at the young age of 44 he was more often thought of as a pornographer but in the ensuing years he has come to be more rightly regarded as one of the most imaginative writers these shores have produced. As well as his novels and plays he was also a masterful poet and wrote over 800 of them. In this collection we discover and nourish ourselves on a small part of that legacy that reveals much about the man and his views on life.

Many of the poems are also available as an audiobook from our sister company Portable Poetry. Many samples are at our youtube channel http://www.youtube.com/user/PortablePoetry?feature=mhee The full volume can be purchased from iTunes, Amazon and other digital stores. Among our readers are Richard Mitchley and Ghizela Rowe

Index Of Poems

Letter from Town: On a Grey Morning in March
Afternoon in School
Bei Hennef
Excursion
New Year's Eve
Piano
Rose Of All The World
The Mosquito
Conundrums
The Mess of Love
Discord in Childhood
Week-Night Service
Last Words To Miriam
Piccadilly Circus At Night: Street-Walkers
Brother And Sister
Dreams Old
Discipline
Hyde Park At Night, Before The War Clerks.
Whales Weep Not!
Figs
Tortise Shout
Rose Of All The World
Excursion
New Heaven And Earth

Snake
The Drained Cup
Bare Almond trees
Eagle In New Mexico
Wages
Humming Bird

Letter from Town: On a Grey Morning in March
The clouds are pushing in grey reluctance slowly northward to you,
While north of them all, at the farthest ends, stands one
bright-bosomed, aglance with fire as it guards the wild north cloud-coasts, red-fire
seas running through the rocks where ravens flying to windward melt as a well-shot lance.

You should be out by the orchard, where violets secretly darken the earth,
Or there in the woods of the twilight, with northern wind-flowers shaken astir.
Think of me here in the library, trying and trying a song that is worth
Tears and swords to my heart, arrows no armour will turn or deter.

You tell me the lambs have come, they lie like daisies white in the grass
Of the dark-green hills; new calves in shed; peewits turn after the plough -
It is well for you. For me the navvies work in the road where I pass
And I want to smite in anger the barren rock of each waterless brow.

Like the sough of a wind that is caught up high in the mesh of the budding trees,
A sudden car goes sweeping past, and I strain my soul to hear
The voice of the furtive triumphant engine as it rushes past like a breeze,
To hear on its mocking triumphance unwitting the after-echo of fear.

Afternoon in School
The Last Lesson
When will the bell ring, and end this weariness?
How long have they tugged the leash, and strained apart
My pack of unruly hounds: I cannot start
Them again on a quarry of knowledge they hate to hunt,
I can haul them and urge them no more.
No more can I endure to bear the brunt
Of the books that lie out on the desks: a full three score
Of several insults of blotted pages and scrawl
Of slovenly work that they have offered me.
I am sick, and tired more than any thrall
Upon the woodstacks working weariedly.

And shall I take
The last dear fuel and heap it on my soul
Till I rouse my will like a fire to consume
Their dross of indifference, and burn the scroll
Of their insults in punishment? - I will not!
I will not waste myself to embers for them,
Not all for them shall the fires of my life be hot,

For myself a heap of ashes of weariness, till sleep
Shall have raked the embers clear: I will keep
Some of my strength for myself, for if I should sell
It all for them, I should hate them
I will sit and wait for the bell.

Bei Hennef
The little river twittering in the twilight,
The wan, wondering look of the pale sky,
This is almost bliss.

And everything shut up and gone to sleep,
All the troubles and anxieties and pain
Gone under the twilight.

Only the twilight now, and the soft "Sh!" of the river
That will last for ever.

And at last I know my love for you is here;
I can see it all, it is whole like the twilight,
It is large, so large, I could not see it before,
Because of the little lights and flickers and interruptions,
Troubles, anxieties and pains.

You are the call and I am the answer,
You are the wish, and I the fulfilment,
You are the night, and I the day.
What else - it is perfect enough.
It is perfectly complete,
You and I,
What more?

Strange, how we suffer in spite of this.

Excursion
I wonder, can the night go by;
Can this shot arrow of travel fly
Shaft-golden with light, sheer into the sky
Of a dawned to-morrow,
Without ever sleep delivering us
From each other, or loosing the dolorous
Unfruitful sorrow!

What is it then that you can see
That at the window endlessly
You watch the red sparks whirl and flee
And the night look through?
Your presence peering lonelily there
Oppresses me so, I can hardly bear

To share the train with you.

You hurt my heart-beats' privacy;
I wish I could put you away from me;
I suffocate in this intimacy,
For all that I love you;
How I have longed for this night in the train,
Yet now every fibre of me cries in pain
To God to remove you.

But surely my soul's best dream is still
That one night pouring down shall swill
Us away in an utter sleep, until
We are one, smooth-rounded.
Yet closely bitten in to me
Is this armour of stiff reluctancy
That keeps me impounded.

So, dear love, when another night
Pours on us, lift your fingers white
And strip me naked, touch me light,
Light, light all over.
For I ache most earnestly for your touch,
Yet I cannot move, however much
I would be your lover.

Night after night with a blemish of day
Unblown and unblossomed has withered away;
Come another night, come a new night, say
Will you pluck me apart?
Will you open the amorous, aching bud
Of my body, and loose the burning flood
That would leap to you from my heart?

New Year's Eve
There are only two things now,
The great black night scooped out
And this fire-glow.

This fire-glow, the core,
And we the two ripe pips
That are held in store.

Listen, the darkness rings
As it circulates round our fire.
Take off your things.

Your shoulders, your bruised throat!
Your breasts, your nakedness!
This fiery coat!

As the darkness flickers and dips,
As the firelight falls and leaps
From your feet to your lips!

Piano

Softly, in the dusk, a woman is singing to me;
Taking me back down the vista of years, till I see
A child sitting under the piano, in the boom of the tingling strings
And pressing the small, poised feet of a mother who smiles as she sings.

In spite of myself, the insidious mastery of song
Betrays me back, till the heart of me weeps to belong
To the old Sunday evenings at home, with winter outside
And hymns in the cosy parlour, the tinkling piano our guide.

So now it is vain for the singer to burst into clamour
With the great black piano appassionato. The glamour
Of childish days is upon me, my manhood is cast
Down in the flood of remembrance, I weep like a child for the past.

I am here myself; as though this heave of effort
At starting other life, fulfilled my own;
Rose-leaves that whirl in colour round a core
Of seed-specks kindled lately and softly blown

Rose Of All The World

By all the blood of the rose-bush into being -
Strange, that the urgent will in me, to set
My mouth on hers in kisses, and so softly
To bring together two strange sparks, beget

Another life from our lives, so should send
The innermost fire of my own dim soul out-spinning
And whirling in blossom of flame and being upon me!
That my completion of manhood should be the beginning

Another life from mine! For so it looks.
The seed is purpose, blossom accident.
The seed is all in all, the blossom lent
To crown the triumph of this new descent.

Is that it, woman? Does it strike you so?
The Great Breath blowing a tiny seed of fire
Fans out your petals for excess of flame,
Till all your being smokes with fine desire?

Or are we kindled, you and I, to be
One rose of wonderment upon the tree

Of perfect life, and is our possible seed
But the residuum of the ecstasy?

How will you have it? - the rose is all in all,
Or the ripe rose-fruits of the luscious fall?
The sharp begetting, or the child begot?
Our consummation matters, or does it not?

To me it seems the seed is just left over
From the red rose-flowers' fiery transience;
Just orts and slarts; berries that smoulder in the bush
Which burnt just now with marvellous immanence.

Blossom, my darling, blossom, be a rose
Of roses unchidden and purposeless; a rose
For rosiness only, without an ulterior motive;
For me it is more than enough if the flower unclose.

The Mosquito
When did you start your tricks,
Monsieur ?

What do you stand on such high legs for ?
Why this length of shredded shank,
You exaltation ?

Is it so that you shall lift your centre of gravity upwards
And weigh no more than air as you alight upon me,
Stand upon me weightless, you phantom ?

I heard a woman call you the Winged Victory
In sluggish Venice.
You turn your head towards your tail, and smile.

How can you put so much devilry
Into that translucent phantom shred
Of a frail corpus ?

Queer, with your thin wings and your streaming legs
How you sail like a heron, or a dull clot of air,
A nothingness.

Yet what an aura surrounds you ;
Your evil little aura, prowling, and casting a numbness on my mind.

That is your trick, your bit of filthy magic :
Invisibility, and the anæsthetic power
To deaden my attention in your direction.
But I know your game now, streaky sorcerer.

Queer, how you stalk and prowl the air
In circles and evasions, enveloping me,
Ghoul on wings Winged Victory.

 Settle, and stand on long thin shanks
Eyeing me sideways, and cunningly conscious that I am aware,
You speck.

I hate the way you lurch off sideways into air
Having read my thoughts against you.

Come then, let us play at unawares,
And see who wins in this sly game of bluff,
Man or mosquito.

You don't know that I exist, and I don't know that you exist.
Now then !

It is your trump,
It is your hateful little trump,
You pointed fiend,
Which shakes my sudden blood to hatred of you :
It is your small, high, hateful bugle in my ear.

Why do you do it ?
Surely it is bad policy.

They say you can't help it.

If that is so, then I believe a little in Providence protecting the innocent.
But it sounds so amazingly like a slogan,
A yell of triumph as you snatch my scalp.

Blood, red blood
Super-magical
Forbidden liquor.

I behold you stand
For a second enspasmed in oblivion,
Obscenely estasied
Sucking live blood,
My blood.

Such silence, such suspended transport,
Such gorging,
Such obscenity of trespass.

You stagger
As well as you may.
Only your accursed hairy frailty,
Your own imponderable weightlessness

Saves you, wafts you away on the very draught my anger makes in its snatching.

Away with a pæan of derision,
You winged blood-drop.

Can I not overtake you ?
Are you one too many for me,
Winged Victory ?
Am I not mosquito enough to out-mosquito you?

Queer, what a big stain my sucked blood makes
Beside the infinitesimal faint smear of you !
Queer, what a dim dark smudge you have disappeared into !

Conundrums
Tell me a word
that you've often heard,
yet it makes you squint
when you see it in print!

Tell me a thing
that you've often seen
yet if put in a book
it makes you turn green!

Tell me a thing
that you often do,
when described in a story
shocks you through and through!

Tell me what's wrong
with words or with you
that you don't mind the thing
yet the name is taboo.

The Mess of Love
We've made a great mess of love
since we made an ideal of it.
 The moment I swear to love a woman, a certain woman, all my life
that moment I begin to hate her.
The moment I even say to a woman: I love you! -
my love dies down considerably.
The moment love is an understood thing between us, we are sure of it,
it's a cold egg, it isn't love any more.
Love is like a flower, it must flower and fade;
if it doesn't fade, it is not a flower,
it's either an artificial rag blossom, or an immortelle, for the cemetery.
The moment the mind interferes with love, or the will fixes on it,
or the personality assumes it as an attribute, or the ego takes possession of it,

it is not love any more, it's just a mess.
And we've made a great mess of love, mind-perverted, will-perverted, ego-perverted love.

Discord in Childhood
Outside the house an ash-tree hung its terrible whips,
And at night when the wind arose, the lash of the tree
Shrieked and slashed the wind, as a ship's
Weird rigging in a storm shrieks hideously.

Within the house two voices arose in anger, a slender lash
Whistling delirious rage, and the dreadful sound
Of a thick lash booming and bruising, until it drowned
The other voice in a silence of blood, 'neath the noise of the ash.
How Beastly The Bourgeois Is
How beastly the bourgeois is
especially the male of the species—
Presentable, eminently presentable—
shall I make you a present of him?

Isn't he handsome? Isn't he healthy? Isn't he a fine specimen?
Doesn't he look the fresh clean Englishman, outside?
Isn't it God's own image? tramping his thirty miles a day
after partridges, or a little rubber ball?
wouldn't you like to be like that, well off, and quite the thing

Oh, but wait!
Let him meet a new emotion, let him be faced
with another man's need,
let him come home to a bit of moral difficulty, let life
face him with a new demand on his understanding
and then watch him go soggy, like a wet meringue.
Watch him turn into a mess, either a fool or a bully.
Just watch the display of him, confronted with a new
demand on his intelligence,
a new life-demand.
How beastly the bourgeois is
especially the male of the species

Nicely groomed, like a mushroom
standing there so sleek and erect and eyeable
and like a fungus, living on the remains of a bygone life
sucking his life out of the dead leaves of greater life
than his own.
And even so, he's stale, he's been there too long.
Touch him, and you'll find he's all gone inside
just like an old mushroom, all wormy inside, and hollow
under a smooth skin and an upright appearance.
Full of seething, wormy, hollow feelings
rather nasty—
How beastly the bourgeois is!

Standing in their thousands, these appearances, in damp England
what a pity they can't all be kicked over
like sickening toadstools, and left to melt back, swiftly
into the soil of England.

Week-Night Service
The five old bells
Are hurrying and eagerly calling,
Imploring, protesting
They know, but clamorously falling
Into gabbling incoherence, never resting,
Like spattering showers from a bursten sky-rocket dropping
In splashes of sound, endlessly, never stopping.
The silver moon
That somebody has spun so high
To settle the question, yes or no, has caught
In the net of the night's balloon,
And sits with a smooth bland smile up there in the sky
Smiling at naught,
Unless the winking star that keeps her company
Makes little jests at the bells' insanity,
As if he knew aught!
The patient Night
Sits indifferent, hugged in her rags,
She neither knows nor cares
Why the old church sobs and brags;
The light distresses her eyes, and tears
Her old blue cloak, as she crouches and covers her face,
Smiling, perhaps, if we knew it, at the bells' loud clattering disgrace.
 The wise old trees
Drop their leaves with a faint, sharp hiss of contempt,
While a car at the end of the street goes by with a laugh;
As by degrees
The poor bells cease, and the Night is exempt,
And the stars can chaff
The ironic moon at their ease, while the dim old church
Is peopled with shadows and sounds and ghosts that lurchby:

Last Words To Miriam
Yours is the shame and sorrow
But the disgrace is mine;
Your love was dark and thorough,
Mine was the love of the sun for a flower
He creates with his shine.

I was diligent to explore you,
Blossom you stalk by stalk,
Till my fire of creation bore you

Shrivelling down in the final dour
Anguish—then I suffered a balk.

I knew your pain, and it broke
My fine, craftsman's nerve;
Your body quailed at my stroke,
And my courage failed to give you the last
Fine torture you did deserve.

You are shapely, you are adorned,
But opaque and dull in the flesh,
Who, had I but pierced with the thorned
Fire-threshing anguish, were fused and cast
In a lovely illumined mesh.

Like a painted window: the best
Suffering burnt through your flesh,
Undrossed it and left it blest
With a quivering sweet wisdom of grace: but now
Who shall take you afresh?

Now who will burn you free
From your body's terrors and dross,
Since the fire has failed in me?
What man will stoop in your flesh to plough
The shrieking cross?

A mute, nearly beautiful thing
Is your face, that fills me with shame
As I see it hardening,
Warping the perfect image of God,
And darkening my eternal fame.

Piccadilly Circus At Night: Street-Walkers
When into the night the yellow light is roused like dust above the towns,
Or like a mist the moon has kissed from off a pool in the midst of the downs,

Our faces flower for a little hour pale and uncertain along the street,
Daisies that waken all mistaken white-spread in expectancy to meet

The luminous mist which the poor things wist was dawn arriving across the sky,
When dawn is far behind the star the dust-lit town has driven so high.

All the birds are folded in a silent ball of sleep,
All the flowers are faded from the asphalt isle in the sea,

Only we hard-faced creatures go round and round, and keep
The shores of this innermost ocean alive and illusory.

Wanton sparrows that twittered when morning looked in at their eyes

And the Cyprian's pavement-roses are gone, and now it is we

Flowers of illusion who shine in our gauds, make a Paradise
On the shores of this ceaseless ocean, gay birds of the town-dark sea.

Brother And Sister

The shorn moon trembling indistinct on her path,
Frail as a scar upon the pale blue sky,
Draws towards the downward slope: some sorrow hath
Worn her down to the quick, so she faintly fares
Along her foot-searched way without knowing why
She creeps persistent down the sky's long stairs.

Some day they see, though I have never seen,
The dead moon heaped within the new moon's arms;
For surely the fragile, fine young thing had been
Too heavily burdened to mount the heavens so.
But my heart stands still, as a new, strong dread alarms
Me; might a young girl be heaped with such shadow of woe?

Since Death from the mother moon has pared us down to the quick,
And cast us forth like shorn, thin moons, to travel
An uncharted way among the myriad thick
Strewn stars of silent people, and luminous litter
Of lives which sorrows like mischievous dark mice chavel
To nought, diminishing each star's glitter,

Since Death has delivered us utterly, naked and white,
Since the month of childhood is over, and we stand alone,
Since the beloved, faded moon that set us alight
Is delivered from us and pays no heed though we moan
In sorrow, since we stand in bewilderment, strange
And fearful to sally forth down the sky's long range.

We may not cry to her still to sustain us here,
We may not hold her shadow back from the dark.
Oh, let us here forget, let us take the sheer
Unknown that lies before us, bearing the ark
Of the covenant onwards where she cannot go.
Let us rise and leave her now, she will never know.

Dreams Old

I have opened the window to warm my hands on the sill
Where the sunlight soaks in the stone: the afternoon
Is full of dreams, my love, the boys are all still
In a wistful dream of Lorna Doone.

The clink of the shunting engines is sharp and fine,
Like savage music striking far off, and there

On the great, uplifted blue palace, lights stir and shine
Where the glass is domed in the blue, soft air.

There lies the world, my darling, full of wonder and wistfulness and strange
Recognition and greetings of half-acquaint things, as I greet the cloud
Of blue palace aloft there, among misty indefinite dreams that range
At the back of my life's horizon, where the dreamings of past lives crowd.

Over the nearness of Norwood Hill, through the mellow veil
Of the afternoon glows to me the old romance of David and Dora,
With the old, sweet, soothing tears, and laughter that shakes the sail
Of the ship of the soul over seas where dreamed dreams lure the unoceaned explorer.

All the bygone, hushèd years
Streaming back where the mist distils
Into forgetfulness: soft-sailing waters where fears
No longer shake, where the silk sail fills
With an unfelt breeze that ebbs over the seas, where the storm
Of living has passed, on and on
Through the coloured iridescence that swims in the warm
Wake of the tumult now spent and gone,
Drifts my boat, wistfully lapsing after
The mists of vanishing tears and the echo of laughter.

Discipline

It is stormy, and raindrops cling like silver bees to the pane,
The thin sycamores in the playground are swinging with flattened leaves;
The heads of the boys move dimly through a yellow gloom that stains
The class; over them all the dark net of my discipline weaves.

It is no good, dear, gentleness and forbearance, I endured too long:
I have pushed my hands in the dark soil, under the flower of my soul
And the gentle leaves, and have felt where the roots are strong
Fixed in the darkness, grappling for the deep soil's little control.

And there is the dark, my darling, where the roots are entangled and fight
Each one for its hold on the oblivious darkness, I know that there
In the night where we first have being, before we rise on the light,
We are not brothers, my darling, we fight and we do not spare.

And in the original dark the roots cannot keep, cannot know
Any communion whatever, but they bind themselves on to the dark,
And drawing the darkness together, crush from it a twilight, a slow
Burning that breaks at last into leaves and a flower's bright spark.

I came to the boys with love, my dear, but they turned on me;
I came with gentleness, with my heart 'twixt my hands like a bowl,
Like a loving-cup, like a grail, but they spilt it triumphantly
And tried to break the vessel, and to violate my soul.

But what have I to do with the boys, deep down in my soul, my love?
I throw from out of the darkness my self like a flower into sight,
Like a flower from out of the night-time, I lift my face, and those
Who will may warm their hands at me, comfort this night.

But whosoever would pluck apart my flowering shall burn their hands,
So flowers are tender folk, and roots can only hide,
Yet my flowerings of love are a fire, and the scarlet brands
Of my love are roses to look at, but flames to chide.

But comfort me, my love, now the fires are low,
Now I am broken to earth like a winter destroyed, and all
Myself but a knowledge of roots, of roots in the dark that throw
A net on the undersoil, which lies passive beneath their thrall.

But comfort me, for henceforth my love is yours alone,
To you alone will I offer the bowl, to you will I give
My essence only, but love me, and I will atone
To you for my general loving, atone as long as I live.

Hyde Park At Night, Before The War Clerks.
We have shut the doors behind us, and the velvet flowers of night
Lean about us scattering their pollen grains of golden light.

Now at last we lift our faces, and our faces come aflower
To the night that takes us willing, liberates us to the hour.

Now at last the ink and dudgeon passes from our fervent eyes
And out of the chambered weariness wanders a spirit abroad on its enterprise.

Not too near and not too far
Out of the stress of the crowd
Music screams as elephants scream
When they lift their trunks and scream aloud
For joy of the night when masters are
Asleep and adream.

So here I hide in the Shalimar
With a wanton princess slender and proud,
And we swoon with kisses, swoon till we seem
Two streaming peacocks gone in a cloud
Of golden dust, with star after star
On our stream.

Whales Weep Not!
They say the sea is cold, but the sea contains
the hottest blood of all, and the wildest, the most urgent.
All the whales in the wider deeps, hot are they, as they urge
on and on, and dive beneath the icebergs.

The right whales, the sperm-whales, the hammer-heads, the killers
there they blow, there they blow, hot wild white breath out of the sea!

And they rock, and they rock, through the sensual ageless ages
on the depths of the seven seas,
and through the salt they reel with drunk delight
and in the tropics tremble they with love
and roll with massive, strong desire, like gods.
Then the great bull lies up against his bride
in the blue deep bed of the sea,
as mountain pressing on mountain, in the zest of life:
and out of the inward roaring of the inner red ocean of whale-blood
the long tip reaches strong, intense, like the maelstrom-tip, and comes to rest
in the clasp and the soft, wild clutch of a she-whale's fathomless body.

And over the bridge of the whale's strong phallus, linking the   wonder of whales
the burning archangels under the sea keep passing, back and forth,
keep passing, archangels of bliss
from him to her, from her to him, great Cherubim
that wait on whales in mid-ocean, suspended in the waves of the sea
great heaven of whales in the waters, old hierarchies.

And enormous mother whales lie dreaming suckling their whale- tender young
and dreaming with strange whale eyes wide open in the waters of the beginning and the end.

And bull-whales gather their women and whale-calves in a ring
when danger threatens, on the surface of the ceaseless flood
and range themselves like great fierce Seraphim facing the threat
encircling their huddled monsters of love.

And all this happens in the sea, in the salt
where God is also love, but without words:
and Aphrodite is the wife of whales
most happy, happy she!

and Venus among the fishes skips and is a she-dolphin
she is the gay, delighted porpoise sporting with love and the sea
she is the female tunny-fish, round and happy among the males
and dense with happy blood, dark rainbow bliss in the sea.

Figs
The proper way to eat a fig, in society,
Is to split it in four, holding it by the stump,
And open it, so that it is a glittering, rosy, moist, honied, heavy-petalled
four-petalled flower.

Then you throw away the skin
Which is just like a four-sepalled calyx,
After you have taken off the blossom, with your lips.

But the vulgar way
Is just to put your mouth to the crack, and take out the flesh in one bite.

Every fruit has its secret.

The fig is a very secretive fruit.
As you see it standing growing, you feel at once it is symbolic :
And it seems male.
But when you come to know it better, you agree with the Romans, it is female.

The Italians vulgarly say, it stands for the female part ; the fig-fruit :
The fissure, the yoni,
The wonderful moist conductivity towards the centre.

Involved,
Inturned,
The flowering all inward and womb-fibrilled ;
And but one orifice.

The fig, the horse-shoe, the squash-blossom.
Symbols.

There was a flower that flowered inward, womb-ward ;
Now there is a fruit like a ripe womb.

It was always a secret.
That's how it should be, the female should always be secret.

There never was any standing aloft and unfolded on a bough
Like other flowers, in a revelation of petals ;
Silver-pink peach, venetian green glass of medlars and sorb-apples,
Shallow wine-cups on short, bulging stems
Openly pledging heaven :
Here's to the thorn in flower ! Here is to Utterance !
The brave, adventurous rosaceæ.

Folded upon itself, and secret unutterable,
And milky-sapped, sap that curdles milk and makes ricotta,
Sap that smells strange on your fingers, that even goats won't taste it ;
Folded upon itself, enclosed like any Mohammedan woman,
Its nakedness all within-walls, its flowering forever unseen,
One small way of access only, and this close-curtained from the light ;
Fig, fruit of the female mystery, covert and inward,
Mediterranean fruit, with your covert nakedness,
Where everything happens invisible, flowering and fertilization, and fruiting
In the inwardness of your you, that eye will never see
Till it's finished, and you're over-ripe, and you burst to give up your ghost.

Till the drop of ripeness exudes,
And the year is over.

And then the fig has kept her secret long enough.
So it explodes, and you see through the fissure the scarlet.
And the fig is finished, the year is over.

That's how the fig dies, showing her crimson through the purple slit
Like a wound, the exposure of her secret, on the open day.
Like a prostitute, the bursten fig, making a show of her secret.

That's how women die too.

The year is fallen over-ripe,
The year of our women.
The year of our women is fallen over-ripe.
The secret is laid bare.
And rottenness soon sets in.
The year of our women is fallen over-ripe.

When Eve once knew in her mind that she was naked
She quickly sewed fig-leaves, and sewed the same for the man.
She'd been naked all her days before,
But till then, till that apple of knowledge, she hadn't had the fact on her mind.

She got the fact on her mind, and quickly sewed fig-leaves.
And women have been sewing ever since.
But now they stitch to adorn the bursten fig, not to cover it.
They have their nakedness more than ever on their mind,
And they won't let us forget it.

Now, the secret
Becomes an affirmation through moist, scarlet lips
That laugh at the Lord's indignation.

What then, good Lord ! cry the women.
We have kept our secret long enough.
We are a ripe fig.
Let us burst into affirmation.

They forget, ripe figs won't keep.
Ripe figs won't keep.

Honey-white figs of the north, black figs with scarlet inside, of the south.
Ripe figs won't keep, won't keep in any clime.
What then, when women the world over have all bursten into affirmation ?
And bursten figs won't keep ?

The Ship of Death by DH Lawrence
I
Now it is autumn and the falling fruit
and the long journey towards oblivion.

The apples falling like great drops of dew
to bruise themselves an exit from themselves.

And it is time to go, to bid farewell
to one's own self, and find an exit
from the fallen self.

II
Have you built your ship of death, O have you?
O build your ship of death, for you will need it.

The grim frost is at hand, when the apples will fall
thick, almost thundrous, on the hardened earth.

And death is on the air like a smell of ashes!
Ah! can't you smell it?

And in the bruised body, the frightened soul
finds itself shrinking, wincing from the cold
that blows upon it through the orifices.

III
And can a man his own quietus make
with a bare bodkin?

With daggers, bodkins, bullets, man can make
a bruise or break of exit for his life;
but is that a quietus, O tell me, is it quietus?

Surely not so! for how could murder, even self-murder
ever a quietus make?

IV
O let us talk of quiet that we know,
that we can know, the deep and lovely quiet
of a strong heart at peace!

How can we this, our own quietus, make?

V
Build then the ship of death, for you must take
the longest journey, to oblivion.

And die the death, the long and painful death
that lies between the old self and the new.

Already our bodies are fallen, bruised, badly bruised,
already our souls are oozing through the exit
of the cruel bruise.

Already the dark and endless ocean of the end

is washing in through the breaches of our wounds,
already the flood is upon us.

Oh build your ship of death, your little ark
and furnish it with food, with little cakes, and wine
for the dark flight down oblivion.

VI
Piecemeal the body dies, and the timid soul
has her footing washed away, as the dark flood rises.

We are dying, we are dying, we are all of us dying
and nothing will stay the death-flood rising within us
and soon it will rise on the world, on the outside world.

We are dying, we are dying, piecemeal our bodies are dying
and our strength leaves us,
and our soul cowers naked in the dark rain over the flood,
cowering in the last branches of the tree of our life.

VII
We are dying, we are dying, so all we can do
is now to be willing to die, and to build the ship
of death to carry the soul on the longest journey.

A little ship, with oars and food
and little dishes, and all accoutrements
fitting and ready for the departing soul.

Now launch the small ship, now as the body dies
and life departs, launch out, the fragile soul
in the fragile ship of courage, the ark of faith
with its store of food and little cooking pans
and change of clothes,
upon the flood's black waste
upon the waters of the end
upon the sea of death, where still we sail
darkly, for we cannot steer, and have no port.

There is no port, there is nowhere to go
only the deepening black darkening still
blacker upon the soundless, ungurgling flood
darkness at one with darkness, up and down
and sideways utterly dark, so there is no direction any more
and the little ship is there; yet she is gone.
She is not seen, for there is nothing to see her by.
She is gone! gone! and yet
somewhere she is there.
Nowhere!

VIII

And everything is gone, the body is gone
completely under, gone, entirely gone.
The upper darkness is heavy as the lower,
between them the little ship
is gone
she is gone.

It is the end, it is oblivion.

IX
And yet out of eternity a thread
separates itself on the blackness,
a horizontal thread
that fumes a little with pallor upon the dark.

Is it illusion? or does the pallor fume
A little higher?
Ah wait, wait, for there's the dawn,
the cruel dawn of coming back to life out of oblivion.

Wait, wait, the little ship
drifting, beneath the deathly ashy grey of a flood-dawn.

Wait, wait! even so, a flush of yellow
and strangely, O chilled wan soul, a flush of rose.
A flush of rose, and the whole thing starts again.

X
The flood subsides, and the body, like a worn sea-shell
emerges strange and lovely.
And the little ship wings home, faltering and lapsing on the pink flood,

and the frail soul steps out, into the house again
filling the heart with peace.

Swings the heart renewed with peace even of oblivion.

Oh build your ship of death, oh build it!
for you will need it.
For the voyage of oblivion awaits you.

Tortise Shout
I thought he was dumb,
I said he was dumb,
Yet I've heard him cry.

First faint scream,
Out of life's unfathomable dawn,
Far off, so far, like a madness, under the horizon's dawning rim,
Far, far off, far scream.

Tortoise in extremis.
Why were we crucified into sex?
Why were we not left rounded off, and finished in ourselves,
As we began,
As he certainly began, so perfectly alone?

A far, was-it-audible scream,
Or did it sound on the plasm direct?
Worse than the cry of the new-born,
A scream,
A yell,
A shout,
A pæan,
A death-agony,
A birth-cry,
A submission,
All tiny, tiny, far away, reptile under the first dawn.

War-cry, triumph, acute-delight, death-scream reptilian,
Why was the veil torn?
The silken shriek of the soul's torn membrane?
The male soul's membrane
Torn with a shriek half music, half horror.

Crucifixion.
Male tortoise, cleaving behind the hovel-wall of that dense female,
Mounted and tense, spread-eagle, out-reaching out of the shell
In tortoise-nakedness,
Long neck, and long vulnerable limbs extruded, spread-eagle over her house-roof,
And the deep, secret, all-penetrating tail curved beneath her walls,
Reaching and gripping tense, more reaching anguish in uttermost tension
Till suddenly, in the spasm of coition, tupping like a jerking leap, and oh!
Opening its clenched face from his outstretched neck
And giving that fragile yell, that scream,
Super-audible,
From his pink, cleft, old-man's mouth,
Giving up the ghost,
Or screaming in Pentecost, receiving the ghost.

His scream, and his moment's subsidence,
The moment of eternal silence,
Yet unreleased, and after the moment, the sudden, startling jerk of coition, and at once
The inexpressible faint yell
And so on, till the last plasm of my body was melted back
To the primeval rudiments of life, and the secret.
So he tups, and screams
Time after time that frail, torn scream
After each jerk, the longish interval,
The tortoise eternity,
Agelong, reptilian persistence,

Heart-throb, slow heart-throb, persistent for the next spasm.
I remember, when I was a boy,
I heard the scream of a frog, which was caught with his foot in the mouth of an up-starting snake;
I remember when I first heard bull-frogs break into sound in the spring;
I remember hearing a wild goose out of the throat of night
Cry loudly, beyond the lake of waters;
I remember the first time, out of a bush in the darkness, a nightingale's piercing cries and gurgles startled the depths of my soul;
I remember the scream of a rabbit as I went through a wood at midnight;
I remember the heifer in her heat, blorting and blorting through the hours, persistent and irrepressible;
I remember my first terror hearing the howl of weird, amorous cats;
I remember the scream of a terrified, injured horse, the sheet-lightning
And running away from the sound of a woman in labor, something like an owl whooing,
And listening inwardly to the first bleat of a lamb,
The first wail of an infant,
And my mother singing to herself,
And the first tenor singing of the passionate throat of a young collier, who has long since drunk himself to death,
The first elements of foreign speech
On wild dark lips.

And more than all these,
And less than all these,
This last,
Strange, faint coition yell
Of the male tortoise at extremity,
Tiny from under the very edge of the farthest far-off horizon of life.

The cross,
The wheel on which our silence first is broken,
Sex, which breaks up our integrity, our single inviolability, our deep silence
Tearing a cry from us.
Sex, which breaks us into voice, sets us calling across the deeps, calling, calling for the complement,
Singing, and calling, and singing again, being answered, having found.
Torn, to become whole again, after long seeking for what is lost,
The same cry from the tortoise as from Christ, the Osiris-cry of abandonment,
That which is whole, torn asunder,
That which is in part, finding its whole again throughout the universe.

Rose Of All The World
I am here myself; as though this heave of effort
At starting other life, fulfilled my own;
Rose-leaves that whirl in colour round a core
Of seed-specks kindled lately and softly blown

By all the blood of the rose-bush into being -
Strange, that the urgent will in me, to set
My mouth on hers in kisses, and so softly
To bring together two strange sparks, beget

Another life from our lives, so should send
The innermost fire of my own dim soul out-spinning
And whirling in blossom of flame and being upon me!
That my completion of manhood should be the beginning

Another life from mine! For so it looks.
The seed is purpose, blossom accident.
The seed is all in all, the blossom lent
To crown the triumph of this new descent.

Is that it, woman? Does it strike you so?
The Great Breath blowing a tiny seed of fire
Fans out your petals for excess of flame,
Till all your being smokes with fine desire?

Or are we kindled, you and I, to be
One rose of wonderment upon the tree
Of perfect life, and is our possible seed
But the residuum of the ecstasy?

How will you have it? - the rose is all in all,
Or the ripe rose-fruits of the luscious fall?
The sharp begetting, or the child begot?
Our consummation matters, or does it not?

To me it seems the seed is just left over
From the red rose-flowers' fiery transience;
Just orts and slarts; berries that smoulder in the bush
Which burnt just now with marvellous immanence.

Blossom, my darling, blossom, be a rose
Of roses unchidden and purposeless; a rose
For rosiness only, without an ulterior motive;
For me it is more than enough if the flower unclose.

Excursion
I wonder, can the night go by;
Can this shot arrow of travel fly
Shaft-golden with light, sheer into the sky
Of a dawned to-morrow,
Without ever sleep delivering us
From each other, or loosing the dolorous
Unfruitful sorrow!

What is it then that you can see
That at the window endlessly
You watch the red sparks whirl and flee
And the night look through?
Your presence peering lonelily there

Oppresses me so, I can hardly bear
To share the train with you.

You hurt my heart-beats' privacy;
I wish I could put you away from me;
I suffocate in this intimacy,
For all that I love you;
How I have longed for this night in the train,
Yet now every fibre of me cries in pain
To God to remove you.

But surely my soul's best dream is still
That one night pouring down shall swill
Us away in an utter sleep, until
We are one, smooth-rounded.
Yet closely bitten in to me
Is this armour of stiff reluctancy
That keeps me impounded.

So, dear love, when another night
Pours on us, lift your fingers white
And strip me naked, touch me light,
Light, light all over.
For I ache most earnestly for your touch,
Yet I cannot move, however much
I would be your lover.

Night after night with a blemish of day
Unblown and unblossomed has withered away;
Come another night, come a new night, say
Will you pluck me apart?
Will you open the amorous, aching bud
Of my body, and loose the burning flood
That would leap to you from my heart?

New Heaven And Earth

I

And so I cross into another world
shyly and in homage linger for an invitation
from this unknown that I would trespass on.
I am very glad, and all alone in the world,
all alone, and very glad, in a new world
where I am disembarked at last.
I could cry with joy, because I am in the new world, just ventured in.
I could cry with joy, and quite freely, there is nobody to know.
And whosoever the unknown people of this unknown world may be
they will never understand my weeping for joy to be adventuring among them
because it will still be a gesture of the old world I am making
which they will not understand, because it is quite, quite foreign to them.

II
I was so weary of the world
I was so sick of it
everything was tainted with myself,
skies, trees, flowers, birds, water,
people, houses, streets, vehicles, machines,
nations, armies, war, peace-talking,
work, recreation, governing, anarchy,
it was all tainted with myself, I knew it all to start with
because it was all myself.

When I gathered flowers, I knew it was myself plucking my own flowering.
When I went in a train, I knew it was myself travelling by my own invention.
When I heard the cannon of the war, I listened with my own ears to my own destruction.
When I saw the torn dead, I knew it was my own torn dead body.
It was all me, I had done it all in my own flesh.

III
I shall never forget the maniacal horror of it all in the end
when everything was me, I knew it all already, I anticipated it all in my soul
because I was the author and the result
I was the God and the creation at once;
creator, I looked at my creation;
created, I looked at myself, the creator:
it was a maniacal horror in the end.
I was a lover, I kissed the woman I loved,
and God of horror, I was kissing also myself.
I was a father and a begetter of children,
and oh, oh horror, I was begetting and conceiving in my own body.

IV
At last came death, sufficiency of death,
and that at last relieved me, I died.
I buried my beloved; it was good, I buried myself and was gone.
War came, and every hand raised to murder;
very good, very good, every hand raised to murder!
Very good, very good, I am a murderer!
It is good, I can murder and murder, and see them fall
the mutilated, horror-struck youths, a multitude
one on another, and then in clusters together
smashed, all oozing with blood, and burned in heaps
going up in a foetid smoke to get rid of them
the murdered bodies of youths and men in heaps
and heaps and heaps and horrible reeking heaps
till it is almost enough, till I am reduced perhaps;
thousands and thousands of gaping, hideous foul dead
that are youths and men and me
being burned with oil, and consumed in corrupt
thick smoke, that rolls
and taints and blackens the sky, till at last it is dark, dark as night, or death, or hell
and I am dead, and trodden to nought in the smoke-sodden tomb;

dead and trodden to nought in the sour black earth
of the tomb; dead and trodden to nought, trodden to nought.

V
God, but it is good to have died and been trodden out
trodden to nought in sour, dead earth
quite to nought
absolutely to nothing
nothing   nothing   nothing.
For when it is quite, quite nothing, then it is everything.
When I am trodden quite out, quite, quite out
every vestige gone, then I am here
risen, and setting my foot on another world
risen, accomplishing a resurrection
risen, not born again, but risen, body the same as before,
new beyond knowledge of newness, alive beyond life
proud beyond inkling or furthest conception of pride
living where life was never yet dreamed of, nor hinted at
here, in the other world, still terrestrial
myself, the same as before, yet unaccountably new.

VI
I, in the sour black tomb, trodden to absolute death
I put out my hand in the night, one night, and my hand
touched that which was verily not me
verily it was not me.
Where I had been was a sudden blaze
a sudden flaring blaze!
So I put my hand out further, a little further
and I felt that which was not I,
it verily was not I
it was the unknown.
Ha, I was a blaze leaping up!
I was a tiger bursting into sunlight.
I was greedy, I was mad for the unknown.
I, new-risen, resurrected, starved from the tomb
starved from a life of devouring always myself
now here was I, new-awakened, with my hand stretching out
and touching the unknown, the real unknown, the unknown unknown.
My God, but I can only say
I touch, I feel the unknown!
I am the first comer!
Cortes, Pisarro, Columbus, Cabot, they are nothing, nothing!
I am the first comer!
I am the discoverer!
I have found the other world!
The unknown, the unknown!
I am thrown upon the shore.
I am covering myself with the sand.
I am filling my mouth with the earth.
I am burrowing my body into the soil.

The unknown, the new world!

VII
It was the flank of my wife
I touched with my hand, I clutched with my hand
rising, new-awakened from the tomb!
It was the flank of my wife
whom I married years ago
at whose side I have lain for over a thousand nights
and all that previous while, she was I, she was I;
I touched her, it was I who touched and I who was touched.
Yet rising from the tomb, from the black oblivion
stretching out my hand, my hand flung like a drowned man's hand on a rock,
I touched her flank and knew I was carried by the current in death
over to the new world, and was climbing out on the shore,
risen, not to the old world, the old, changeless I, the old life,
wakened not to the old knowledge
but to a new earth, a new I, a new knowledge, a new world of time.
Ah no, I cannot tell you what it is, the new world
I cannot tell you the mad, astounded rapture of its discovery.
I shall be mad with delight before I have done,
and whosoever comes after will find me in the new world
a madman in rapture.

VIII
Green streams that flow from the innermost continent of the new world,
what are they?
Green and illumined and travelling for ever
dissolved with the mystery of the innermost heart of the continent
mystery beyond knowledge or endurance, so sumptuous
out of the well-heads of the new world.--
The other, she too has strange green eyes!
White sands and fruits unknown and perfumes that never
can blow across the dark seas to our usual world!
And land that beats with a pulse!
And valleys that draw close in love!
And strange ways where I fall into oblivion of uttermost living!--
Also she who is the other has strange-mounded
breasts and strange sheer slopes, and white levels.
Sightless and strong oblivion in utter life takes possession of me!
The unknown, strong current of life supreme
drowns me and sweeps me away and holds me down
to the sources of mystery, in the depths,
extinguishes there my risen resurrected life
and kindles it further at the core of utter mystery.

Snake
A snake came to my water-trough
On a hot, hot day, and I in pyjamas for the heat,
To drink there.

In the deep, strange-scented shade of the great dark carob-tree
I came down the steps with my pitcher
And must wait, must stand and wait, for there he was at the trough before me.
He reached down from a fissure in the earth-wall in the gloom
And trailed his yellow-brown slackness soft-bellied down, over the edge of the stone trough
And rested his throat upon the stone bottom,
i o And where the water had dripped from the tap, in a small clearness,
He sipped with his straight mouth,
Softly drank through his straight gums, into his slack long body,
Silently.
Someone was before me at my water-trough,
And I, like a second comer, waiting.
He lifted his head from his drinking, as cattle do,
And looked at me vaguely, as drinking cattle do,
And flickered his two-forked tongue from his lips, and mused a moment,
And stooped and drank a little more,
Being earth-brown, earth-golden from the burning bowels of the earth
On the day of Sicilian July, with Etna smoking.
The voice of my education said to me
He must be killed,
For in Sicily the black, black snakes are innocent, the gold are venomous.
And voices in me said, If you were a man
You would take a stick and break him now, and finish him off.
But must I confess how I liked him,
How glad I was he had come like a guest in quiet, to drink at my water-trough
And depart peaceful, pacified, and thankless,
Into the burning bowels of this earth?
Was it cowardice, that I dared not kill him?
Was it perversity, that I longed to talk to him? Was it humility, to feel so honoured?
I felt so honoured.
And yet those voices:
If you were not afraid, you would kill him!
And truly I was afraid, I was most afraid, But even so, honoured still more
That he should seek my hospitality
From out the dark door of the secret earth.
He drank enough
And lifted his head, dreamily, as one who has drunken,
And flickered his tongue like a forked night on the air, so black,
Seeming to lick his lips,
And looked around like a god, unseeing, into the air,
And slowly turned his head,
And slowly, very slowly, as if thrice adream,
Proceeded to draw his slow length curving round
And climb again the broken bank of my wall-face.
And as he put his head into that dreadful hole,
And as he slowly drew up, snake-easing his shoulders, and entered farther,
A sort of horror, a sort of protest against his withdrawing into that horrid black hole,
Deliberately going into the blackness, and slowly drawing himself after,
Overcame me now his back was turned.

I looked round, I put down my pitcher,
I picked up a clumsy log
And threw it at the water-trough with a clatter.
I think it did not hit him,
But suddenly that part of him that was left behind convulsed in undignified haste.
Writhed like lightning, and was gone
Into the black hole, the earth-lipped fissure in the wall-front,
At which, in the intense still noon, I stared with fascination.
And immediately I regretted it.
I thought how paltry, how vulgar, what a mean act!
I despised myself and the voices of my accursed human education.
And I thought of the albatross
And I wished he would come back, my snake.
For he seemed to me again like a king,
Like a king in exile, uncrowned in the underworld,
Now due to be crowned again.
And so, I missed my chance with one of the lords
Of life.
And I have something to expiate:
A pettiness.

The Drained Cup

T' snow is witherin' off 'n th' gress—
Lad, should I tell thee summat?
T' snow is witherin' off 'n th' gress
An' mist is suckin' at th' spots o' snow,
An' ower a' the thaw an' mess
There's a moon, full blow.
Lad, but I'm tellin' thee summat!
Tha's bin snowed up i' this cottage wi' me—
'Ark, tha'rt for hearin' summat!
Tha's bin snowed up i' this cottage wi' me
While t' clocks 'as 'a run down an' stopped,
An' t' short days goin' unknown ter thee
Unbeknown has dropped.
Yi, but I'm tellin' thee summat.
How many days dost think has gone?
Now, lad, I'm axin' thee summat.
How many days dost think has gone?
How many times has t' candle-light shone
On thy face as tha got more white an' wan?
Seven days, my lad, or none!
Aren't ter hearin' summat?
Tha come ter say good-bye ter me,
Tha wert frit o' summat.
Tha come ter ha' finished an' done wi' me
An' off to a gel as wor younger than me,
An' fresh and more nicer for marryin' wi'—
Yi, but tha'rt frit o' summat.

Ah wunna kiss thee, tha trembles so!
Tha'rt daunted, or summat.
Tha arena very flig ter go.
Dost want meter want thee again? Nay, though,
There's hardly owt left o' thee; get up and go!
Or dear o' me, say summat.
Tha wanted ter leave me that bad, tha knows!
Doesn't ter know it?
But tha wanted me more ter want thee, so's
Tha could let thy very soul out. A man
Like thee can't rest till his last spunk goes
Out of 'im into a woman as can
Draw it out of 'im. Did ter know it?
Tha thought tha wanted a little wench,
Ay, lad, I'll tell thee thy mind.
Tha thought tha wanted a little wench
As 'ud make thee a wife an' look up ter thee.
As 'ud wince when that touched'er close, an' blench
An' lie frightened to death under thee.
She worn't hard ter find.
Tha thought tha wanted ter be rid o' me.
'Appen tha did, an' a'.
Tha thought tha wanted ter marry an' see
If ter couldna be master an' th' woman's boss.
Tha'd need a woman different from me,
An' tha knowed it; ay, yet tha comes across
Ter say good-bye! an' a'.

I tell thee tha won't be satisfied,
Tha might as well listen, tha knows.
I tell thee tha won't be satisfied
Till a woman has drawn the last last drop
O' thy spunk, an' tha'rt empty 'an mortified.
Empty an empty from bottom to top.
It's true, tha knows.

Tha'rt one o' th' men as has got to drain
An' I've loved thee for it,
Their blood in a woman, to the very lasy vein,
Tha must, though tha tries ter get away.
Tha wants it, and everything else is in vain.
An' a woman like me loves thee for it.
Maun tha cling to the wa' as that stands?
Ay, an' tha maun.
An' tha looks at me, an' tha understan's.
Yi, tha can go. Tha hates me now.
But tha'lt come again. Because when a man's
Not finished, he hasn't, no matter how.
Go then, sin' tha maun.
Tha come ter say good-bye ter me.
Now go then, now then go.

It's ta'en thee seven days ter say it ter me.
Now go an' marry that wench an' see
How long it'll be afore tha'lt be
Weary an' sick o' the likes o' she,
An' hankerin' for me. But go!
A woman's man tha art, ma lad.
But it's my sort o' woman.
Go then, tha'lt ha'e no peace till ter's had
A go at t'other, for I'm a bad a bad
Sort o' woman for any lad.
Ay, it's a rum un!

Bare Almond trees
Wet almond-trees, in the rain,
Like iron sticking grimly out of earth ;
Black almond trunks, in the rain,
Like iron implements twisted, hideous, out of the earth,
Out of the deep, soft fledge of Sicilian winter-green,
Earth-grass uneatable,
Almond trunks curving blackly, iron-dark, climbing the slopes.

Almond-tree, beneath the terrace rail,
Black, rusted, iron trunk,
You have welded your thin stems finer,
Like steel, like sensitive steel in the air,
Grey, lavender, sensitive steel, curving thinly and brittly up in a parabola.
What are you doing in the December rain ?
Have you a strange electric sensitiveness in your steel tips ?
Do you feel the air for electric influences
Like some strange magnetic apparatus ?
Do you take in messages, in some strange code,
From heaven's wolfish, wandering electricity, that prowls so constantly round Etna ?
Do you take the whisper of sulphur from the air ?
Do you hear the chemical accents of the sun ?
Do you telephone the roar of the waters over the earth ?
And from all this, do you make calculations ?

Sicily, December's Sicily in a mass of rain
With iron branching blackly, rusted like old, twisted implements
And brandishing and stooping over earth's wintry fledge, climbing the slopes
Of uneatable soft green !

Eagle In New Mexico
Towards the sun, towards the south-west
A scorched breast.
A scorched breast, breasting the sun like an answer,
Like a retort.
An eagle at the top of a low cedar-bush
On the sage-ash desert

Reflecting the scorch of the sun from his breast;
Eagle, with the sickle dripping darkly above.

Erect, scorched-pallid out of the hair of the cedar,
Erect, with the god-thrust entering him from below,
Eagle gloved in feathers
In scorched white feathers
In burnt dark feathers
In feathers still fire-rusted ;
Sickle-overswept, sickle dripping over and above.

Sun-breaster,
Staring two ways at once, to right and left ;
Masked-one
Dark-visaged
Sickle-masked
With iron between your two eyes ;
You feather-gloved
To the feet ;
Foot-fierce ;
Erect one ;
The god-thrust entering you steadily from below.

You never look at the sun with your two eyes.
Only the inner eye of your scorched broad breast
Looks straight at the sun.

You are dark
Except scorch-pale-breasted ;
And dark cleaves down and weapon-hard downward curving
At your scorched breast,
Like a sword of Damocles,
Beaked eagle.

You've dipped it in blood so many times
That dark face-weapon, to temper it well,
Blood-thirsty bird.
Why do you front the sun so obstinately,
American eagle ?
As if you owed him an old, old grudge, great sun : or an old, old allegiance.

When you pick the red smoky heart from a rabbit or a light-blooded bird
Do you lift it to the sun, as the Aztec priests used to lift red hearts of men ?

Does the sun need steam of blood do you think
In America, still,
Old eagle ?

Does the sun in New Mexico sail like a fiery bird of prey in the sky
Hovering ?

Does he shriek for blood ?
Does he fan great wings above the prairie, like a hovering, blood-thirsty bird ?

And are you his priest, big eagle
Whom the Indians aspire to ?
Is there a bond of bloodshed between you ?

Is your continent cold from the ice-age still, that the sun is so angry ?
Is the blood of your continent somewhat reptilian still,
That the sun should be greedy for it ?

I don't yield to you, big, jowl-faced eagle
Nor you nor your blood-thirsty sun
That sucks up blood
Leaving a nervous people.

Fly off, big bird with a big black back.
Fly slowly away, with a rust of fire in your tail,
Dark as you are on your dark side, eagle of heaven.

Even the sun in heaven can be curbed and chastened at last
By the life in the hearts of men.
And you, great bird, sun-starer, heavy black beak
Can be put out of office as sacrifice bringer.

Wages

The wages of work is cash.
The wages of cash is want more cash.
The wages of want more cash is vicious competition.
The wages of vicious competition is – the world we live in.

The work-cash-want circle is the viciousest circle
that ever turned men into fiends.

Earning a wage is a prison occupation
and a wage-earner is a sort of gaol-bird.

Earning a salary is a prison overseer's job
a gaoler instead of a gaol-bird.

Living on our income is strolling grandly outside the prison
in terror lest you have to go in. And since the work-prison covers
almost every scrap of the living earth, you stroll up and down
on a narrow beat, about the same as a prisoner taking exercise.

This is called universal freedom.

Humming Bird

I can imagine, in some otherworld

Primeval-dumb, far back
In that most awful stillness, that only gasped and hummed,
Humming-birds raced down the avenues.

Before anything had a soul,
While life was a heave of Matter, half inanimate,
This little bit chipped off in brilliance
And went whizzing through the slow, vast, succulent stems.

I believe there were no flowers, then,
In the world where the humming-bird flashed ahead of creation.
I believe he pierced the slow vegetable veins with his long beak.

Probably he was big
As mosses, and little lizards, they say were once big.
Probably he was a jabbing, terrifying monster.
We look at him through the wrong end of the long telescope of Time,
Luckily for us.

www.ingramcontent.com/pod-product-compliance
Lightning Source LLC
Chambersburg PA
CBHW061314040426
42444CB00010B/2639